The Mind of A Winner

"Here is the teenager's guide to winning in life."

"Winning is a choice and it all starts with the decisions and choices you make today because your present choices will shape your future outcome."

Dexter & Petula Jones

Foreword by Jasmine Shonte' Jones

UWriteIt Publishing Company
Goldsboro, NC USA
www.uwriteitpublishingcompany.com
www.wewaituntilmarriage.org

The Mind of A Winner by Dexter & Petula Jones
Copyright © 2011 by Dexter & Petula Jones
ALL RIGHTS RESERVED

ISBN: **ISBN-13: 978-0615554525**
ISBN-10: 0615554520

First Printing October 2011

NO PART OF THIS BOOK MAY BE REPRODUCED IN ANY FORM, BY PHOTOCOPYING OR BY ANY ELECTRONIC OR MECHANICAL MEANS, INCLUDING INFORMATION STORAGE OR RETRIEVAL SYSTEMS, WITHOUT PERMISSION IN WRITING FROM THE COPYRIGHT OWNERS/AUTHOR.

Unless otherwise indicated, Scripture quotations in this book are from the King James Version of the Bible.

This publication is designed to provide information in regard to the subject matter covered. It is published with the understanding that the authors are not engaged in rendering legal counsel or other professional services. If legal advice or other professional advice is required, the services of a professional person should be sought.

Printed in the U.S.A.

Dedication – Dexter L. Jones

We are truly thankful to God for blessing us with the desire to educate, inform and inspire youths to become all that they can be. The teens of today are the future of tomorrow and it is given to us to shape that future by example, mentorship and becoming all that we can be as a witness to the truth that righteousness prevails. As always I dedicate this book to my precious daughter Jasmine Shonte' Jones, a daughter that I am so proud of and that I love so dearly. Jasmine, I am so proud of you and the example that you display in word, deed and truth as a testimony to other teens that they can be whatever they put their mind to, Daddy.

Also, to my son Brandon, I dedicate this book to you even though you are no longer a teen, in your teen years you displayed leadership abilities and have gone on to become a young man that I am so proud of, Mother.

Contents

Introduction

1. The Winner's Circle
2. The Mind
3. Potential and Purpose
4. Choices
5. The Mind of A Winner
6. Honor Your Parents
7. Abstinence versus Celibacy
8. Current Statistics and Facts
9. The Spiritual Minded Teen
10. True Friendship
11. A Boyfriend or Girlfriend

Foreword
By
Jasmine Jones

My name is Jasmine Jones and I am the daughter of the author of this inspirational self-help book. I am in the 11th grade and I attend Wayne Early Middle College High School. I am sixteen years old and highly motivated toward my future. Day by day as I try to carry out my goals I always remember that "I am a Winner." I have carried this message with me along with my faith in God throughout my school years. As a result, I can name many accomplishments I have simply because of the mindset I have kept of a winner.

Beginning in kindergarten I have always made 'principal's list' and kept an A average. In the eighth grade, God blessed me and I was given recognition with a promise award for conveying promise toward my future and the leadership in academic accomplishments. In 2008, recognition as 'Miss Scholarship' in a pageant called, P.E.A.R.L.S, which was a group of young girls that participated in community activities and promoting self-etiquette and high self-esteem. In 2011 I took part in one of my biggest accomplishments yet, this is when I help co-founded and help coördinated an organization called "Fashion4TheFuture." My partner and I held a fashion show for young girls (ages 7-12) that incorporated dance and freedom of expression in fashion to promote high self-esteem, confidence, and well-rounded character. I must say, this fashion show wouldn't have been a complete success if I had not had the mindset of a winner.

This book will not only tell you how-to be a winner but it explains to you why you should-be, while covering heart to heart struggles teens like you and I endure throughout our daily lives. As teens we may think the world doesn't comprehend our emotions, we may think the world is careless or unaware of our being, or simply think that they know what we should do with OUR lives. This book tackles all that and more, guiding us on how to relieve ourselves from those worldly restrictions to become future leaders and fulfill our purpose in life and do God's will.

This book discusses sex, relationships, abstinence, family quarrels, drama from friends, school, grades, being a teen of God and acceptance from your peers, and even the oppression of a parent-adolescent relationship. This book teaches us we can conquer all things through Christ along with the knowledge to make better choices for ourselves. "The Mind of a Winner" will not try to turn you into the perfect teen but it will transform your mind into the perfect place to make decisions for yourself. To be a winner read this book and I'm sure your mindset will change for the better.

Sincerely,
Jasmine Jones

A Word from Dexter & Petula Jones

We are the founders of WAIT, an organization that's focused on celibacy as the only 100 percent effective way to preventing pregnancy and contracting STD. Our goal is to educate and share with teens through educational and inspirational programs geared toward promoting knowledge and inspiration to wait.

We do this by reinforcing self-confidence and positive values, goals, dreams, purpose and attitudes as an important prerequisite. We are available for seminars and workshops at schools, churches, after-school programs, teen-retreats, etc. We also teach about relationship building, STD, pregnancy, and celibacy. The time has come to take back our teens through inspiration and education and eventually celebration as we see our teens that are sexually active go from being sexually active to celibacy with the idea to abstain from all sexual activity until marriage. And those that are virgins remaining so until their wedding day.

Introduction

You are a winner in life and within you is potential to do great things. You're created for greatness and the determining factor of whether you will be or not is your attitude. Your mind is the battlefield and if you want to win in life you must have the mind of a winner. Your attitude will decide your altitude. Therefore, you must get control of your mind, you must get control of your emotions, you must get control of your actions and then you will win in life. Winning is a choice and it all starts with the decisions and choices you make today, in this book we will show you how to have and apply the mind of a winner.

Truly, this is the book that can change your life, you may meet opposition that will try to hinder you from reading this book. One of the most enlightening chapters in this book is chapter 5, **be determined to read to the end of chapter 5** and your mind will never be the same again. You may want to immediately go to chapter 5, don't do this because you will miss out on the wisdom of the first four chapters. This book is the truth and it will set you free, no matter what your past may have been get ready to enter the winner's circle.

1
The Winner's Circle

"In life 5% of the people in the world controls 95% of the world's wealth and are the major players and decision makers on earth."

The winner's circle consists of those that are achievers. To be a part of the winner's circle you must be around those that are winners. You will find in life that winners associate with other winners, winners do not associate with losers. To be a part of the winner's circle is to have the winner's attitude. You can decide whether you are walking with a winner or not by noticing their attitude and way of speech. The attitude of a winner is:

- **Spiritual**
- **Positive**
- **Resolute**
- **Optimistic**
- **Encouraging**
- **Upbeat**
- **Confident**
- **Motivating**
- **Selfless**

Those that are part of the winner's circle are people who will inspire and urge you in your daily walk. They will bring to you a good report and let you know that you can do it, you can make it and you can meet your goals in life. In the scriptures we have the story of 13 people who went to go out and search the land to bring back a report of the conditions of the land. Two of the people were winners and a part of the winner's circle, the remaining eleven were losers and were negative about the land.

So it goes, " *AND THE LORD, spake unto Moses, saying, Send thou men, that they may search out the land of Canaan, which I give unto the children of Israel: of every tribe of their fathers shall ye send a man, every one a ruler among them. And Moses sent them to spy out the land of Canaan, and said unto them, Get you up this way southward, and go up into the mountain: And see the land, what it is; and the people that dwelleth therein, whether they be strong or weak, few or many; And what the land is that they dwell in, whether it be good or bad; and what cities they be that they dwell in, whether in tents, or in strong holds.*

And what the land is, whether it be fat or lean, whether there be wood therein, or not.

And be ye of good courage, and bring of the fruit of the land. Now the time was the time of the firstripe grapes. And they returned from searching of the land after forty days. And they went and came to Moses, and to Aaron, and to all the congregation, and showed them the fruit of the land.

And they told him, and said, We came unto the land whither thou sentest us, and surely it floweth with milk and honey; and this is the fruit of it. Nevertheless the people be strong that dwell in the land, and the cities are walled, and very great: and moreover we saw the children of Anak there.

And Caleb stilled the people before Moses, and said, Let us go up at once, and possess it; for we are well able to overcome it. But the men that went up with him said, We be not able to go up against the people (negative thinkers, losers); for they are stronger than we. And they brought up an evil report of the land which they had searched unto the children of Israel, saying, The land, through which we have gone to search it, is a land that eateth up the inhabitants thereof; and all the people that we saw in it are men of a great stature. And there we saw the giants, the sons of Anak, which come of the giants: and we were in our own sight as grasshoppers, and so we were in their sight. AND ALL the congregation lifted up their voice, and cried; and the people wept that night

And the men, which Moses sent to search the land, who returned, and made all the congregation to murmur against him, by bringing up a slander upon the land, Even those men that did bring up the evil report upon the land, died by the plague before the LORD. But Joshua the son of Nun, and Caleb the son of Jephunneh, which were of the men that went to search the land, lived still." Numbers 13-14

The only two that had the attitude of a winner were Joshua and Caleb, these people were a part of the winner's circle and their attitude and way of speech showed forth. The attitudes of losers are an attitude of:

- Negativity
- Carnal
- Pessimist
- Wavering
- Discouragement
- Downtrodden
- Insecure

1. Those that are a part of the winner's circle realize that they are teens of the kingdom. They have the mind of Christ and they refuse to run with negative teens that are going nowhere in life.

2. *Those that are a part of the winner's circle don't allow the losers to influence them in any way. Their mind is on success and they refuse to settle in life.*
3. *Those that are a part of the winner's circle control their own life and refuse to accept the loser's attitude because they know if they do they will become a loser themselves.*
4. *Those that are a part of the winner's circle have a high standard in life while the losers have a low standard.*
5. *Those that are a part of the winner's circle say yes to success and no to failure.*
6. *Those that are a part of the winner's circle are seekers of the kingdom of God and refuse to lower their standard to run with carnal Christians.*
7. *Those that are a part of the winner's circle are diligent in school, they don't do drugs or alcohol, they don't have sex before marriage nor do they allow peer pressure to influence their decisions.*

The loser's circle is totally opposite of the winner's circle and the losers are easily influenced by peer pressure and they will not hearken to instruction, the voice of their parents and they despise wisdom. The scripture gives us warnings about hanging with losers saying, *"The fear of the LORD is the beginning of knowledge: but fools despise wisdom and instruction. My son, hear the instruction of thy father, and forsake not the law of thy mother. For they shall be an ornament of grace unto thy head, and chains about thy neck.*

My son, if sinners entice thee, consent thou not. If they say, Come with us, let us lay wait for blood, let us lurk privily for the innocent without cause: Let us swallow them up alive as the grave; and whole as those that go down into the pit: We shall find all precious substance, we shall fill our houses with spoil: Cast in thy lot among us; let us all have one purse: My son, walk not thou in the way with them; refrain thy foot from their path." Proverbs 1:7-15

- You have to decide that you will be a part of the winner's circle.
- You must realize your worth and refuse to settle for less.
- You must accept the attitude of a winner
- You must realize that you are a part of the kingdom of God.
- You must know that you are special and unique.
- You must know that life is about choices and you will make the right choices.

You are an awesome creature endowed with awesome ability and potential. When you come into the knowledge and understanding of who you are and realize that you are more than meets the eye, you will be a force to reckon with. *"You are fearfully and wonderfully made." Psalms 139:14* If you could be seen as whom you really are you would be seen as an awesome, unbelievable creation full of potential and possibilities.

You are a creation endowed with intelligence and powers beyond your belief. The making of your body and the ability of your soul makes you a creation far above the animal kingdom. You have the God-given intelligence unlike any other creature. Out of all of God's creations, humanity has the most highly developed brains. Your brain is the master nucleus of the body. It consistently receives information from the senses both about the inside and outside of the body. It takes this information and quickly analyzes it, and then sends out messages that control the body actions and functions. The human brain consists of billions of interconnected cells which enable your creativity, use language, plan and solve difficult problems. You are a creation full of potential and possibilities and you are a part of the winner's circle.

- *You are great.*
- *You are full of potential.*
- *You have awesome ability.*
- *You have intelligence.*
- *You are gifted.*
- *You are magnanimous.*
- *You are priceless.*
- *You are powerful.*
- *You are valuable.*
- *You can be whatever you want to be.*

It's time for you to come forth and be the awesome person that you are. But you must first realize that you are full of energy and according to how you channel that energy will decide how successful you will become in life. The best way to channel that energy as a teen is to make God first priority in your life. Second, decide that you are a part of the winner's circle by having the attitude of a winner. Third, focus on your school work, and your dreams and goals in life. As a winner you have gifts and passions in life and these are the tools that will enable you to accomplish great things and fulfill your destiny.

As a winner you must ask yourself the right questions to get the right answers. If you don't know where you're going any road you take will get you there. Here are the questions that winners ask:

1. *What is my gift?*
2. *What is my passion?*
3. *What do I love to do?*
4. *What would I be doing right now as a career?*
5. *What do I dream about doing in life?*

You can begin to take the initiative as a teen to focus on your dreams and goals now. If you want a career as a lawyer you can get your parent or a mentor to take you to the court room to see cases. You can begin to read books and other literature that deals with law, court etc… If you want a career as a fashion designer you can get a sewing machine and begin now to make clothes and other items. You can go online and find out about all the cool things that fashion designers use as well as read books about the subject. Whatever you want focus on learning more about the subject through reading, the internet, seminars and other sources. This will enhance your learning and familiarize you with your passion and gifts.

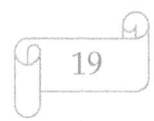

You're created for greatness and to live a fulfilled and satisfying life. You are already wired for the winner's circle you just don't know how to go about possessing that which is already yours. In this book we will take you step by step as promised to unveil to you the wisdom and understanding of how to equip yourself for success in your teen years thereby setting your course for life. In this book we will not leave anything to chance we will guide you to the right way of thinking and planning that are essential for success and winning which are known and used by the successful few. In this book we will lay out the plan that will show you how to win in life. You are one step away from the mind of a winner.

2
The Mind

"The mind is your battlefield, decisions and choices are made within the mind and we see the outcome of your choices manifested in your daily life."

The one idea I want to convey to you in this chapter relates to the thoughts in your mind. As a society we have failed to realize the power of our thoughts, we've failed to realize that the thoughts which dominate our thinking has a direct correlation and connection with the things that we experience in our life. Here are six of the most powerful words that I can relate to you that can change your life.

WE BECOME WHAT WE THINK ABOUT

Where you are right now in your life as a teen is a result of the thoughts that continually dominate your thinking.

- *You cannot wish, hope and desire to do better in school, abstain from sex before marriage, not do drugs and alcohol, have the right kind of friends in your life and then have thoughts of laziness, sex before marriage, wanting to try drugs and alcohol, and desiring to be with the wrong crowd dominating your thought life.*

- *Either one thought pattern or the other will dominate your mind and produce results in accordance with the dominating thoughts you're thinking.*

- *You can't think one way and then expect another way to come forth, the thoughts you're sowing in your mind you will reap in your life and there's no way around it. You will become what you think.*

- *You must come into the knowledge that your thoughts are what you, your teen years and your life will become. There is no exception to this rule you will become the dominating thoughts that you're thinking.*

There is a universal law in the realm of the mind that works the same for all humanity, that law is **"like attract like, cause and effect,** what you sow, you will reap, and everything produces after its kind." An apple tree cannot produce oranges nor can a pecan tree produce plums every tree only produces after its kind. Therefore, you must begin to renew your mind to change your thinking.

- *Your thinking needs to change from failure consciousness to "success consciousness."*

- *Your thinking needs to change from I'm not worthy to "I am more than worthy of the best in life."*

- *Your thinking needs to change from sex before marriage to "celibacy is the only 100 percent effective way to prevent out-of-wedlock pregnancy and STD."*

- *Your thinking needs to change from I'll try this just once to "I will keep my mind and body intact and will not try alcohol and drugs once (or ever again)."*

- *Your thinking needs to change from I can't to" I can do all things through Christ which strengthens me."*

And when you change your thoughts your whole life change. Your thoughts create your circumstances and lifestyle. Your thoughts create images and the image that you consistently hold in your mind will produce for you according to the image of that thought. Man is not a creature of conditions but instead creates his conditions by his dominating thoughts. In essence, what you think you will soon become and as you continue to think so you continue in that state.

The dominating thoughts of your mind that's hidden from others will attract to you the environment and circumstance which your thoughts secretly longs for whether good or bad. We know what you're thinking by the circumstance and situations that surround your life, if you're dissatisfied with the picture your life is portraying to yourself and others then change it by simply changing your thinking. Begin to see yourself not as you are but visualize (or form a mental image of) yourself as if you were what you want to become.

3
Potential and Purpose

"Potential is present but not visible or active power. Its power that lies dormant or inactive, yet within that inactive power lies the ability to make things happen and bring things to pass."

Within an apple is the potential to make a forest of apple trees, the potential is the seeds within the apple. A person can take the seeds of the apple and cast them aside thereby potentially forfeiting an entire forest of apple trees from coming up, or they can plant the seeds from the apple and start an orchard. The orchard lies hidden within the apple but the seed is what will bring the orchard forth. The apple is the main object but the seed is the potential, the water and soil helps the seed to come forth and make it capable of producing an apple tree. Yet, God is the one that gives the increase and causes it to flourish. An apple without seeds cannot produce more apple trees because the potential to do it is gone. Without potential nothing happens yet with potential comes possibilities, potential is latent power or power under the surface that can manifest to come forth into that which you want to see happen. That which you wish to see happen comes from that which you already have.

- *Potential makes things possible, achievable, accessible and obtainable.*

- *Potential has within it the ability to bring things to pass.*

Truly, you are more than meets the eye, as a teenager you are full of potential and possibilities. You can become whatever you want to become in life and the only limitations are those which you acknowledge in your own mind. Every person that went on to do great things in life once upon a time was a teenager with goals and dreams but they went on to carry out those dreams and made the world a better place. Whatever you want to become, within you is the potential to do it, and you can make all your dreams come true. You can become:

- *The President of the United States.*
- *A Fashioner Designer*
- *A Writer*
- *A Lawyer*
- *A Pastor*

- *A Great Business Person*
- *A Great Athlete*
- *A Teacher*
- *A Doctor*
- *A Principal*
- *A Registered Nurse*
- *A Youth Counselor*
- *A Scientist or Chemist*
- *An Economist*
- *An Artist*
- *An Engineer*
- *A Librarian*
- *A Musician*
- *A Secretary*
- *And many other career choices to numerous to list.*

Within you is that seed like the seed within that apple, the seeds are your talents and gifts that you were born with and what you do with them will decide what you will give to the world? Every person is endowed from the creator with a magnificent talent and gift that can bring about a change in their life and the lives of others. Every person is gifted and assigned a purpose to fulfill in the earth. God has placed every individual's destiny in their hands and according to the decision they make they help to orchestrate that destiny. When you

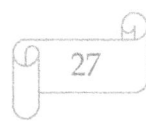

make the right decisions in life, it empowers you to do the impossible. Right thinking produce right decisions, wrong thinking produce wrong decisions, a person's thinking shows forth their thoughts, a person's thoughts bring forth their actions and a person's actions creates their destiny. One of your greatest needs today as a teen is to come to realize your sense of destiny and the original intent of why you are here.

- *You did not come into this world by accident, chance or even mistakenly.*

- *You did not arrive here empty without purpose, without intent, without a reason already placed in you to fulfill and carry out.*

- *You arrived here with a purpose designed for the uplifting of humanity.*

- *You arrived here with something to do, something to impart, something to leave behind.*

- *God put purpose in you while you were still in your mother's womb. Jeremiah 1:5*

When you discover your purpose it will bring happiness, success, prosperity, direction, value, and focus to your own life and to every person you meet. A sad but true statement is that the riches place in the world is neither the oil wells in Texas nor a combination of all the banks and loan companies combined. The riches place in the world is the local cemeteries in our own towns and cities because:

1. *Many people have departed taking with them that song that was never recorded.*

2. *That invention that was never invented.*

3. *Those goals and dreams that were never fulfilled and accomplished.*

4. *That business plan that was never developed etc...*

All these things could have brought success, happiness, and prosperity to those people and countless others if they would have realized their potential and found their purpose.

- **Your purpose is the reason for your existence.**

- Your purpose is the master motivator for your own life.

- Your purpose is who you are.

- Your purpose is why you are.

- Your purpose was the original intent in the mind of God when he allowed you to come to planet earth.

- Your purpose is you.

The power of potential and purpose has within it the ability to change the world, and the next generation of change is depending upon you.

4
Choices

"The choice we make find our future and creates our destiny, for destiny is not a matter of chance but it's by the choices you make."

As a teen these are your most precious years and let it be your aim to make the most of your time by establishing a relationship with God, focusing on your school work and the pursuit of your dreams and goals. Success in life starts with YOU; the choices you make today will decide the outcome of your tomorrows. You are the artist of your own destiny and you can paint the picture according to how you want your future to become.

Ultimately, you create what you want by the decisions that you make and the choices that you take. You can become whatever you want to become in life but the journey along the way is filled with choices that will either side-track you, throw you off course all together or keep you on the path of success. One of the greatest choices that you will have to make as a teen is the decision to have sex or practice a life of celibacy in your teen years. The wrong decision can prevent you from accomplishing your goals in life and cause you to become a statistic on the teen pregnancy and STD chart. Also, for the male teen the wrong decision can have heavy physical and emotional costs and cause you to become a parent before you're ready. However, the right decision can have great rewards for you and help keep you on the right course to pursue your dreams and goals without obligations and responsibilities to hold you back.

As a teen you'll be confronted with many decisions that can cause you success or be a stumbling block in your path. You will be confronted with choices such as:

- *Whether to drink or not to drink.*
- *Whether to do drugs or not to do drugs.*
- *Whether to have sex or remain celibate.*
- *Whether to take school seriously or waste your time.*
- *Choosing the right friends that will be good or bad for you.*
- *Whether you allow self-appreciation or low self-esteem to rule your life.*

In your teen years curiosity is normal, but you must make it your business and goal to practice self-control. Your teen years are precious and you must make it your aim to keep your mind and body intact throughout your teen life. As a teen you have the power to change your life today by the decisions you make and thereby make a great tomorrow for the rest of your life.

Don't become a statistics; you are in control of your future. There is so much to do in life and the future is depending on you. You must change these awful statistics and begin to focus on your dreams, goals and the destiny that awaits you. You are a teen with purpose and you are valuable, needed and loved. You have what it takes to become a success instead of a statistic.

1. *Choose to practice celibacy instead of having sex and engaging in sexual activity.*

2. *Choose not to drink instead of drinking.*

3. *Choose to abstain from drugs instead of becoming a partaker.*

4. *Choose to take your school work seriously so you can prepare for your future.*

5. *Decide to wisely choose friends that will encourage and inspire you.*

6. *Know that you are invaluable and of great worth and needed in the world.*

7. *Decide that this is your life and you will make it what you want it to become.*

The right choices give you vision and order for *"without a vision people perish"* without vision you have no goal to work toward no goal to fulfill and as a result, you cast off restraint and do anything. But right choices bring restraint, control and discipline, it gives you meaning and drive in life and it enables you to live a successful and fulfilled life.

- *The right choices are the driving force in the life of the lifeless.*

- *The right choices are the power that will strengthen the weak and aimless.*

- *The right choices empower you with authority that gives you the permission to succeed in life.*

- *The right choices empower you with influence that gives you the confidence to go boldly after your life's aim.*

- *The right choices will produce for you the future of your choosing.*

Your life consists of choices and you have the God-given ability within you to make the right choices and become all that God has designed for you in life.

5
The Mind of a Winner

"Within the mind of a winner is the attitude of gratitude and the belief that they win in life because winning is all about attitude."

To be a true winner in life you must have the mind of a winner. The one person that truly had a winner's mind was Christ. He always had the attitude of gratitude and the belief that he could do all things with God's help. As a teen, *"Let this mind be in you, which was also in Christ Jesus."* Philippians 2:5 The mind of Christ was a mind:

- *Of encouragement.*
- *That's focused.*
- *That exemplified love.*
- *That had fellowship with the Spirit.*
- *That had affection.*
- *That was merciful to others.*

In this chapter we want to not only show you the mind that Christ had but we want to concentrate on one aspect of Christ's mind in particular and that is the mind that's totally focused. Only by having a focused mind can you change your life to show a life that's prepared for accomplishment? Here is a simple and easy to understand formula that will change your life within the next 30 days. All you have to do is follow this brief formula that I will lay out for you and you will begin a process of attracting to your life the attitude that wins. This attitude will be noticed:

1. **By you first.**
2. **By your family members.**
3. **By your classmates.**
4. **By your friends.**
5. **By your associates.**
6. **By your teachers.**
7. **By all those around you.**

The basis of making anything happen for you and turning things around in your life is **belief.**

- **Belief is enough to change any situation**.

- **Belief can enable you to excel in your schoolwork**.

- **Belief can turn bad into good**.

- Belief is the answer to you excelling in sports.

- Belief is the answer to making you feel like a winner.

- Belief is the trampoline that can bounce you into the destiny that you're created to fulfill.

- Belief is the answer to enabling you to resist temptations.

- Belief can do a thousand other things to many to mention.

You are where you are at this very moment because of your belief system about the various aspects of your life. You can give the bad or good that you're experiencing to your belief and the thoughts that dominate your thinking. But beliefs can change from what it is to what you want it. You are the recipient of the strong beliefs that are now dominant in your heart. Change your belief and you change your life. If you've always had problems believing, fear not for with these simple words and a very powerful formula your belief will grow strong and your belief will do for you whatever you need it to do. Belief is one of the laws of Absolutes. An absolute is something which is complete, correct, pure and right. When properly conformed to the law of absolutes will never let you down. However, if you violate the law of absolutes two things will manifest in life. Either you will experience from minor injury to complete chaos occurring. Also, the thing about the law of absolutes is that it is inviolable and self-enforcing, in other words it has a mind of its own and when it's violated it moves into action.

However, when it's obeyed it likewise moves into action to bring forth success and happiness. In life this law works with absolute certainty and infallibility. There is not a person on the face of the earth that the law of absolutes is not working for now. In the area of life that you're experiencing more failure than success, more bad than good and making more wrong decisions than right decisions you have violated the belief law of Absolutes and it is working against you at this very moment instead of for you. But I have the remedy that will change all that and will get you on the side of the law of Absolutes that will work for you without fail. All you have to do is follow the formula for the next 30 days and watch some of the miraculous changes in your life. If you're tired of:

- **Being unable to excel in your schoolwork.**
- **Feeling like a loser.**
- **Being unfocused.**
- **Being addicted or controlled by substance of any kind.**
- **Being on a course that seems to always get you into trouble.**
- **Being sexually involved at a young age.**
- **Being tormented in your mind.**
- **Unable to have a good social life.**
- **Not excelling in sports.**

Then you've been led to the right source of information to change all that and begin your life anew. There is only one need and that is to confess this formula twice a day for the next 30 days. You will need to confess the formula in the morning when you arise and at night right before you go off to sleep. You can even confess them throughout the day as an added benefit. As you confess these words confess them boldly with feelings and conviction. These words will begin to change your thinking and create dominating thoughts that will create circumstances and situations that are relevant to your confession.

Begin to see yourself not as you are but visualize yourself as if you were what you want to become, you can do this by the formula of meditation. Here are five scriptures and a method of mediation that can bring success into your life as a teen. The Bible tells us about the value of meditation saying, *"This book of the law shall not depart out of thy mouth; but thou shalt meditate therein day and night, that thou mayest observe to do according to all that is written therein: for then thou shalt make thy way prosperous, and then thou shalt have good success." Joshua 1:8*

Here is what to do to win in life: Go into a quite place and begin to meditate on these scriptures. The term mediation is defined as: to ponder over, to think and reflect upon. It means to take these scriptures and turn them over in your mind.

"And we know that all things work **together** for good to them that love God, to them who are the called according to his purpose." Romans 8:28

"According as his **divine** power hath given unto us all things that pertain unto life and godliness, through the knowledge of him that hath called us to glory and virtue." 2 Peter 1:3

I will bless the LORD at all times: his **praise** shall continually be in my mouth. Psalms 34:1

"For the LORD giveth **wisdom**: out of his mouth cometh **knowledge** and **understanding**." Proverbs 2:6

"And I will give unto thee the keys of the kingdom of heaven: and whatsoever thou shalt bind **on** earth shall be bound in heaven: and whatsoever thou shalt loose **on** earth shall be loosed in heaven." Matthew 16:19

Start with the scripture in Romans 8:28 repeat this scripture loud two or three times, you will notice that the word **together** is in bold print. Each scripture has a word in bold print in it, these are the words that will change your life and help you to become a winner.

These words will have a powerful effect on your mind and your spirit. Next, do the same with the second scripture in 2 Peter 1:3 repeat this scripture loud two or three times, you will notice that the word **divine** is in bold print.

Likewise, see yourself in your imagination in successful and prosperous situations where you're accomplishing a task that you want to do, or see yourself reaching a goal that you've set for yourself. Imagine it in detail, see the surroundings, feel it, smell it, touch it, hear it, let it be so real that you can taste its outcome. Begin each of these exercises twice daily, watch the effects of what is happening in your life, you will begin to notice change, extraordinary accomplishments, great self-esteem, wise choices, being enlighten, new ideas, awareness, productivity and ambition. These are the changes that are evolving you into that winner. The scripture says, *"Meditate upon these things; give thyself wholly unto them; that thy profiting may appear to all."* 1 Timothy 4:15

Are you up for the challenge?

Do you want to change your life and circumstance bad enough to do this? Want is vital to achieving this and faith without works is dead. You activate your faith by doing it and you prove you want it by following the formula. If you're ready, let's get started with the second part of the formula that you will do.

CONFESS THE FORMULA BELOW:

*TOGETHER DIVINE PRAISE SLOW
LOVE CRYSTAL ON*

*TOGETHER DIVINE PRAISE SLOW
LOVE CRYSTAL ON*

*TOGETHER DIVINE PRAISE SLOW
LOVE CRYSTAL ON*

*TOGETHER DIVINE PRAISE SLOW
LOVE CRYSTAL ON*

*TOGETHER DIVINE PRAISE SLOW
LOVE CRYSTAL ON*

*TOGETHER DIVINE PRAISE SLOW
LOVE CRYSTAL ON*

*TOGETHER DIVINE PRAISE SLOW
LOVE CRYSTAL ON*

*TOGETHER DIVINE PRAISE SLOW
LOVE CRYSTAL ON*

*TOGETHER DIVINE PRAISE SLOW
LOVE CRYSTAL ON*

*TOGETHER DIVINE PRAISE SLOW
LOVE CRYSTAL ON*

*TOGETHER DIVINE PRAISE SLOW
LOVE CRYSTAL ON*

*TOGETHER DIVINE PRAISE SLOW
LOVE CRYSTAL ON*

*TOGETHER DIVINE PRAISE SLOW
LOVE CRYSTAL ON*

*TOGETHER DIVINE PRAISE SLOW
LOVE CRYSTAL ON*

*TOGETHER DIVINE PRAISE SLOW
LOVE CRYSTAL ON*

*TOGETHER DIVINE PRAISE SLOW
LOVE CRYSTAL ON*

*TOGETHER DIVINE PRAISE SLOW
LOVE CRYSTAL ON*

*TOGETHER DIVINE PRAISE SLOW
LOVE CRYSTAL ON*

*TOGETHER DIVINE PRAISE SLOW
LOVE CRYSTAL ON*

*TOGETHER DIVINE PRAISE SLOW
LOVE CRYSTAL ON*

*TOGETHER DIVINE PRAISE SLOW
LOVE CRYSTAL ON*

*TOGETHER DIVINE PRAISE SLOW
LOVE CRYSTAL ON*

*TOGETHER DIVINE PRAISE SLOW
LOVE CRYSTAL ON*

*TOGETHER DIVINE PRAISE SLOW
LOVE CRYSTAL ON*

*TOGETHER DIVINE PRAISE SLOW
LOVE CRYSTAL ON*

*TOGETHER DIVINE PRAISE SLOW
LOVE CRYSTAL ON*

*TOGETHER DIVINE PRAISE SLOW
LOVE CRYSTAL ON*

*TOGETHER DIVINE PRAISE SLOW
LOVE CRYSTAL ON*

END OF READING THE FORMULA

You were born to win not lose. God created humanity and gave them dominion and authority in the earth. Genesis 1:26 Greatness runs through your veins and you were born a winner. You have just forgotten in all the hustle and bustle of life that winning is your birthright and unless you win in life you are living beneath your privilege. You can just as easily win as you can lose and winning begin in your mind because your attitude determines your altitude. Your make up is the makeup of a winner and people are the only creation that has gotten out of sync with who they are. When you confess this formula daily you would have confessed and affirmed the statement "together divine praise slow love crystal on" 56 times a day. Eventually, the meaning of these words will soak in, your belief will grow strong, and the belief will actually make you a winner in life. Your thinking in the past may not have been that of a winner but all that is changing now because you understand that you were born to win.

- **God made a dog to bark therefore he barks.**

- **God made a cat to meow therefore she meows.**

- **God created a fish with the ability to live in the water and this causes them to swim.**

- **God created a bird with wings to fly therefore they flies.**

- **You were born a winner through Jesus Christ therefore you win.**

Reading this formula daily for the next 30 days will get these words in your mind through repetition and it will create belief in your heart and mind and as you think in your heart so you will become. If you ever feel yourself slipping back into your old way of thinking just pick the book back up and go back at it again for the next 30 days and lo and behold you will be back on track. For when you change your thinking you change your life.

A Definition of These Words

- ***Together*** = in sync, oneness, organized, composed.

- **Divine** = to do the extraordinary, the miraculous.
- **Praise** = an expression of approval, commendation or admiration.
- **Slow** = to make wise judgments, truth, patience, insight and good discernment.
- **Love** = selfless, devotion, generous, kindness, acceptance.
- **Crystal** = clarity, precise knowledge, to look to the future with promise.
- **On** = to be more creative, to be productive and ambition, to forbid or allow something to happen.

6
Honor Your Parents

"Honour thy father and mother; which is the first commandment with promise; That it may be well with thee, and thou mayest live long on the earth." Ephesians 6:2-3

As a teen here is a great promise that God has given you, but the promise is base on fulfilling a condition. That condition is that if your honor your parents God will let it go well with you in life and bless you with long life. Many times as teens you think that your parents do not understand what you're going through or the many challenges that you face in life. This is a trick of the devil and a misconception in your mind; don't forget that your parents were also teenagers once. Many of the things that you are going through they also had to face those same challenges, there is nothing new under the sun. Ecclesiastes 1:9-11

As a teen, there were many peer pressures and I also put peer pressure on others to do many things that I understand now are wrong and that God disapprove of. There were times that I did not honor my parents as I should have but God had mercy on me and spared my life. At the age of 16 I gave my life to Christ and

I changed my way of thinking and living. I begin to honor my parents and respect them as the parents that God has put in charge of my life. As a result God has blessed me that life has gone well for me and at this writing I am 46 years of age. Not one time since then have:

- I ever been in trouble with the law?
- I ever had great sickness upon my body.
- I ever taken any kind of drugs or alcohol.
- My parents had to come and get me out of any kind of trouble.
- God ever forsaken or failed me.

When you begin to honor and respect your parents then God will begin to do many things in your life as a teen and well through your older years. Talk to your parents, there are many things which they know and many instructions which they can give you that can save you a lifetime of trouble. In the scriptures Solomon was writing to his son and giving him instructions and wise counsel, telling him to listen to him and obey his mother and father and if he did it will go well with him and God will bless him. If he doesn't then God want be with him because he does not honor his mother and father and this can become a great tragedy.

Here are his words to his son, "*My son, hear the instruction of thy father, and forsake not the law of thy mother: For they shall be an ornament of grace unto thy head, and chains about thy neck. My son, if sinners entice thee, consent thou not. If they say, Come with us, let us lay wait for blood, let us lurk privily for the innocent without cause: Let us swallow them up alive as the grave; and whole, as those that go down into the pit: We shall find all precious substance, we shall fill our houses with spoil: Cast in thy lot among us; let us all have one purse: My son, walk not thou in the way with them; refrain thy foot from their path: For their feet run to evil, and make haste to shed blood. Surely in vain the net is spread in the sight of any bird. And they lay wait for their own blood; they lurk privily for their own lives.*

So are the ways of every one that is greedy of gain; which taketh away the life of the owners thereof. Wisdom crieth without; she uttereth her voice in the streets: She crieth in the chief place of concourse, in the openings of the gates: in the city she uttereth her words, saying, How long, ye simple ones, will ye love simplicity? and the scorners delight in their scorning, and fools hate knowledge? Turn you at my reproof: behold, I will pour out my spirit unto you, I will make known my words unto you. Because I have called, and ye refused; I have stretched out my hand, and no man regarded; But ye have set at nought all my counsel, and would none of my reproof: I also will laugh at your calamity; I will mock when your fear cometh; When your fear cometh as desolation, and your destruction cometh as a whirlwind; when distress and anguish cometh upon you.

Then shall they call upon me, but I will not answer; they shall seek me early, but they shall not find me: For that they hated knowledge, and did not choose the fear of the LORD: They would none of my counsel: they despised all my reproof. Therefore shall they eat of the fruit of their own way, and be filled with their own devices. For the turning away of the simple shall slay them, and the prosperity of fools shall destroy them. But whoso hearkeneth unto me shall dwell safely, and shall be quiet from fear of evil.

My son, if thou wilt receive my words, and hide my commandments with thee; So that thou incline thine ear unto wisdom, and apply thine heart to understanding;

Yea, if thou criest after knowledge, and liftest up thy voice for understanding; If thou seekest her as silver, and searchest for her as for hid treasures; Then shalt thou understand the fear of the LORD, and find the knowledge of God. For the LORD giveth wisdom: out of his mouth cometh knowledge and understanding. He layeth up sound wisdom for the righteous: he is a buckler to them that walk uprightly. He keepeth the paths of judgment, and preserveth the way of his saints. Then shalt thou understand righteousness, and judgment, and equity; yea, every good path.

When wisdom entereth into thine heart, and knowledge is pleasant unto thy soul; Discretion shall preserve thee, understanding shall keep thee: To deliver thee from the way of the evil man, from the man that speaketh froward things; Who leave the paths of uprightness, to walk in the ways of darkness; Who rejoice to do evil, and delight in the frowardness of the wicked; Whose ways are crooked, and they froward in their paths: To deliver thee from the strange woman, even from the stranger which flattereth with her words; Which forsaketh the guide of her youth, and forgetteth the covenant of her God.

For her house inclineth unto death, and her paths unto the dead. None that go unto her return again, neither take they hold of the paths of life. That thou mayest walk in the way of good men, and keep the paths of the righteous. For the upright shall dwell in the land, and the perfect shall remain in it. But the wicked shall be cut off from the earth, and the transgressors shall be rooted out of it. My son, forget not my law; but let thine heart keep my commandments: For length of days, and long life, and peace, shall they add to thee. Let not mercy and truth forsake thee: bind them about thy neck; write them upon the table of thine heart: So shalt thou find favour and good understanding in the sight of God and man. Trust in the LORD with all thine heart; and lean not unto thine own understanding. In all thy ways acknowledge him, and he shall direct thy paths. Be not wise in thine own eyes: fear the LORD, and depart from evil. It shall be health to thy navel, and marrow to thy bones.

Hear, ye children, the instruction of a father, and attend to know understanding. For I give you good doctrine, forsake ye not my law. For I was my father's son, tender and only beloved in the sight of my mother. He taught me also, and said unto me, Let thine heart retain my words: keep my commandments, and live.

Get wisdom, get understanding: forget it not; neither decline from the words of my mouth. Forsake her not, and she shall preserve thee: love her, and she shall keep thee. Wisdom is the principal thing; therefore get wisdom: and with all thy getting get understanding. Exalt her, and she shall promote thee: she shall bring thee to honour, when thou dost embrace her. She shall give to thine head an ornament of grace: a crown of glory shall she deliver to thee. Hear, O my son, and receive my sayings; and the years of thy life shall be many. I have taught thee in the way of wisdom; I have led thee in right paths. When thou goest, thy steps shall not be straitened; and when thou runnest, thou shall not *stumble. Take fast hold of instruction; let her not go: keep her; for she is thy life. Enter not into the path of the wicked, and go not in the way of evil men. Avoid it, pass not by it, turn from it, and pass away. For they sleep not, except they have done mischief; and their sleep is taken away, unless they cause some to fall. For they eat the bread of wickedness, and drink the wine of violence. But the path of the just is as the shining light, that shineth more and more unto the perfect day. The way of the wicked is as darkness: they know not at what they stumble.*

My son, attend to my words; incline thine ear unto my sayings. Let them not depart from thine eyes; keep them in the midst of thine heart. For they are life unto those that find them, and health to all their flesh. Keep thy heart with all diligence; for out of it are the issues of life. Put away from thee a froward mouth, and perverse lips put far from thee. Let thine eyes look right on, and let thine eyelids look straight before thee. Ponder the path of thy feet, and let all thy ways be established. Turn not to the right hand nor to the left: remove thy foot from evil. Proverbs 1-4

Solomon was giving his son good instruction and as parents we want to give you good instructions also. God who is the greatest Father of all has your best interest at heart and he desires that it go well with you in life and that you will have long life. His instructions to you are simply this; *"Honour thy father and mother; which is the first commandment with promise; That it may be well with thee, and thou mayest live long on the earth."* Ephesians 6:2-3

7
Abstinence versus Celibacy

"Abstinence is an effective way to prevent out-of-wedlock pregnancy and STD but this is only the beginning."

Abstinence definition is the avoidance of sexual intercourse in one's life. **Celibacy** is avoidance of all forms of sexual activity. According to statistics and facts which you will read about in the following chapter teenagers are engaging in sexual intercourse daily. There are right decisions and wrong decisions that you'll be confronted with as a teen.

However, the right decision can have great rewards for you and help keep you on the right course to pursue your dreams and goals and fulfill your destiny for greatness. The right decision is celibacy for this is the only 100% effective way to prevent out-of-wedlock pregnancy and STD. Remember, young girls it only take one time or act of sexual intercourse for you to get pregnant and the young man who promised you that he will be with you will not be found. Also, let's not forget those incurable sexual diseases that you may have to live with for the rest of your life for that so called moment of pleasure. Once you make a choice to have sex there are consequences to that action.

What we have discovered is that abstinence alone is not the answer that will prevent teen pregnancy and STD. Many teens according to our research have engaged in sexual intercourse and half of all teens have done oral sex. Even though you may practice abstinence and abstain from sexual intercourse but engage in oral sex you are simply setting yourself up for the opportunity to eventually engage in sexual intercourse. You cannot hold fire to your chest and not be burned; neither can you engage in oral sex without eventually engaging in sexual intercourse.

Young girls, don't allow that boy to pressure you into oral sex to prove your love for him. Young boys, don't allow that girl to persuade you into having oral sex to prove your manhood. The act of oral sex will lead eventually to sexual intercourse with consequences of pregnancy or a STD that you want be ready for. If you say no to sexual intercourse you are not obligated to that person to say yes to oral sex instead as a way to show you care for them. Oral sex is a very intimate form of sexual activity and will lead to sexual intercourse whether you believe it or not. Oral sex is not an innocent sexual activity; it can lead to several infections, including gonorrhea, syphilis, herpes, HIV the virus which causes AIDS and HPV the human papillomavirus, which has been linked to cervical cancer.

Many people may say that abstinence only is not the answer and I agree with that but celibacy is the answer. Celibacy is the missing link which we have omitted in teaching our teens. To tell them to abstain from sexual intercourse without telling them also to abstain from oral sex and all forms of sexual activity is to give them half-truths and half-truths is more harmful than no truth at all. Half truth has the tendency to make you believe that you're doing right but it does not have the power to sustain and produce a positive result.

We must also realize that telling our kids to use condoms and birth control is actually giving our children a license to have sex. I want my teenage daughter educated and informed about teen pregnancy, STD, oral sex and all the consequences that come with engaging in sexual activity. However, I do not want to give her a license to have sex. When you engage in sex outside of marriage it carries many forms of consequences with it, you can get pregnant and attract an STD, but also the fact that when you engage in sexual intercourse a part of that man or woman becomes a part of you. Having sexual intercourse with a person produces an emotional bond during that sexual relationship. When women give birth or have sex they release a chemical called oxytocin that creates like emotional glue that forms a bond between that female and her sexual partner. When you have several sexual partners you are creating an emotional bond with each that occurs inside of you which cannot be undone from a natural perspective.

Also, sex before marriage is fornication which is an act forbidden of God and he says, *"Now the body is not for fornication, but for the Lord; and the Lord for the body. Flee fornication. Every sin that a man doeth is without the body; but he that committeth fornication sinneth against his own body. What? know ye not that your body is the temple of the Holy Ghost which is in you, which ye have of God, and ye are not your own? For ye are bought with a price: therefore glorify God in your body, and in your spirit, which are God's."* 1 Corinthians 6:13b, 18-20

Decide to keep yourself and practice celibacy until marriage, not only is this the only 100%

effective way to prevent pregnancy and STDs but also it equips you when the time comes to fall in love for all the right reasons.

8
Statistics & Facts

"The wrong decision in life can prevent you from accomplishing your goals and cause you to become a statistic on the teen pregnancy and STD chart."

Among youths we have discovered that sexual activity starts as early as middle school. And according to statistics about every 30 seconds a teenage girl becomes pregnant and over 10,000 teens become infected with a STD every day.

HERE ARE THE FACTS

- Each year over one million pregnancies occur among teenagers, **Ages 14-19.**

- About every 30 seconds a teenage girl becomes pregnant in the United States, **Ages 14-17.**

- Over 3 million teenage girls is affected with the HPV disease. **Ages 14-19**

- A condom fails 15% of the time and doesn't prevent HPV at all. Birth control pills have an 8% failure rate.

- Sexual activity starts as early as middle school, **Age 11-14.**

- 1 in 4 teenage girls are infected with some type of STD, **Ages 14-19.**

- Every day in America over 10,000 teens become affected with STD, **Ages 14-19.**

- By age 18, around 65% of women and 68% of men have had sexual intercourse, **Age 13-18.**

A LIST OF SEXUALLY TRANSMITED DISEASES

Here is a brief list of some of the most common STD that teens face along with the most deadly of them all HIV AIDS.

1. **HPV** = Human Papillomavirus = Genital warts usually appear as a small bump or group of bumps in the genital area. An incurable disease.

2. **Chlamydia** = This disease is often known as the "silent" disease in many people and it will not produce any aware symptoms.

3. **Herpes** = Genital herpes are passed on through skin contact with a person infected

with this virus, most often during sex. As to date this is an incurable disease.

4. **Gonorrhea** = This is one of the most commonly sexually transmitted diseases. You can be infected with gonorrhea and have no particular symptoms that will let you know that you are a carrier of this disease.

5. **Hepatitis A** = This disease is the most common of the seven hepatitis and the most serious.

6. **Syphilis** = This is a venereal infectious sexual disease.

7. **HIV AIDS** = A deadly disease that kills with no cure.

"CELIBACY IS THE ONLY 100 PERCENT EFFECTIVE WAY TO PREVENT OUT-OF-WEDLOCK PREGNANCY AND STD."

9
The Spiritual Minded Teen

"For to be carnally minded is death; but to be spiritual minded is life and peace." Romans 8:6

The spiritual minded teen is the teen that makes the word of God their focus in life and in all their decisions. In the life of a spiritual minded teen there are two things that you must do, you must first study and read the word of God. Second, you must have a prayer life so that you can establish a relationship with your Creator and maker.

The scripture says, *"Remember now thy Creator in the days of thy youth, while the evil days come not, nor the years draw nigh, when thou shalt say, I have no pleasure in them." Ecclesiastes 12:1* In this passage of scripture God is simply saying, remember me now while you're young before old age come upon you. I'm begging you remember God while you're in your teen years and God will direct your steps and keep you in the way which you shall go. Psalms 119:133

To be a spiritual minded teen you must *"Study to show yourself approved unto God, a workman that needeth not to be ashamed, rightly dividing the word of truth." 2 Timothy 2:15*

You must get into the word of God for yourself and study to get answers to life situations. The word of God will be your guide and roadmap in life if you will allow it. The scripture says, *"Thy word is a lamp unto my feet, and a light unto my path." Psalms 119:105*

The only way that you can become spiritual minded and cleanse your ways is by knowing the word and doing what the word says. In Psalms 119:9 it says, *"Wherewithal shall a young man (or woman) cleanse his (her) way? By taking heed thereto according to thy word."* You must fall in love with the word of God and esteem it more than anything else in life. The Psalmist said:

- *"I will delight myself in thy statues: I will not forget thy word." Psalms 119:16*

- *"Open thy mine eyes, that I may behold wondrous things out of thy law." Psalms 119:18*

- *"Thy testimonies also are my delight and my counsellors." Psalms 119:24*

- *"O how love I thy law! it is my meditation all the day. Thou through thy commandments hast made me wiser than mine enemies: for they are ever with me. I have more understanding than all my teachers: for thy testimonies are my meditations. I understand more than the ancients, because I keep thy precepts." Psalms 119:97-100*

- *"Therefore I love thy commandments above gold; yea, above fine gold. Therefore I esteem all thy precepts concerning all things to be right; and I hate every false way. Thy testimonies are wonderful: therefore doth my soul keep them. The entrance of thy words giveth light; it giveth understanding unto the simple. I opened my mouth, and panted: for I longed for thy commandments." Psalms 119:127-131*

- *"Thy word is very pure: therefore thy servant loveth it." Psalms 119:13*

- *"Great peace have they which love thy law: and nothing shall offend them." Psalms 119:165*

The word of God will make you a spiritual minded teen that will serve God in truth and holiness and enable you to serve the Lord in righteousness and do the things that please God. The word of God will renew your mind so that you want be a fleshly carnal minded Christian teen but a spiritual minded Christian teen. *"For they that are after the flesh do mind the things of the flesh; but they that are after the Spirit the things of the Spirit. For to be carnally minded is death; but to be spiritually minded is life and peace. Because the carnal mind is enmity against God: for it is not subject to the law of God, neither indeed can be. So then they that are in the flesh cannot please God. But ye are not in the flesh, but in the Spirit, if so be that the Spirit of God dwell in you. Now if any man have not the Spirit of Christ, he is none of his." Romans 8:5-9*

You must make the word of God a priority and prayer must also be a priority in your life. Therefore, you must set up a prayer life so that you can have times of communion with the Father. Prayer is the believer's line of communication with God and helps you to establish a relationship with the Father. When you pray you give God the right to intervene in your life and to help you in your affairs.

Make prayer a priority in your life by establishing a habit of prayer even as the saints in the scriptures made it a priority in their life.

- *David said, "Evening, and morning, and at noon, will I pray, and cry aloud: and he shall hear my voice." Psalms 55:17*

- *Daniel, "kneeled upon his knees three times a day, and prayed, and gave thanks before his God, as he did aforetime." Daniel 6:10*

- *Jesus said, "Men ought always to pray, and not to faint." Luke 18:1*

In order to set up a habit of prayer there are certain things you must do such as:

1. Set aside a time for prayer.

2. Decide on a minimum time for prayer.

3. Be committed and faithful to your prayer time.

4. Know how to put structure in your prayer by *"entering into his gates with thanksgiving, and into his courts with praise: be thankful unto him, and bless his name." Psalms 100:4-5*

5. Other prayer scriptures to help you in prayer; *Matthew 6:6, 1 Timothy 2:1-2, 8, Mark 11:24-26, Romans 8:26-28*

In the scriptures we see several teens that took God at his word and took on the mind of a winner. Our most familiar teen example are the story of the children of Judah, Daniel, Hananiah, Mishael, and Azaria. These teens had "purposed in their heart that they would not defile themselves with the portion of the king's meat, nor with the wine which he drank." Daniel 1: 6-8 You can read the full story of these teens in the entire book of Daniel 1-3, these were spiritual minded teens.

The mind of a winner is a spiritual mind that recognizes no such thing as failure and knows no such reality as impossible. A spiritual minded teen is one on a mission for God and they see themselves as *"the salt of the earth and the light of the world." Matthew 5:13a, 14a* They live by the word of God because they realize that *"Man shall not live by bread alone, but by every word that proceedeth out of the mouth of God." Matthew 4:4* This is your day to take hold of the word of God and establish a relationship with him for yourself.

10
True Friendship

A friend is *one attached to another by respect or affection. One who supports or favours someone or something.* One of the missing ingredients in relationships today is friendship; many times people will become sexually involved even before they become true friends. Not realizing that intimacy isn't going to make a person truly respect or become affectionate toward them, nor will it cause an individual to support or favour them. Here are some things about a true friend.

- *A true friend loves always.*

- *A man who has friends must show himself friendly: and there is a friend that sticks closer than a brother.*

- *Ointment and perfume rejoice the heart: so doth the sweetness of a man's friend by hearty counsel.*

Most people fail to become friends and think that a relationship is a friendship. When it comes to the opposite sex in order for the two of you to become friends with each other you both must first show yourself friendly towards each other in words, deed and in truth.

If you can't show yourself friendly then you will not have an individual in your corner that will stick with you through thick and thin, or good and bad. A true friend will not only tell you the truth even if it hurts, but will also bring you pleasantness and hearty counsel and good advice when needed. A true friend because they are true will not demand that things always be their way, but will be willing to lay down their life (or way of thinking and doing) to keep harmony and peace in the friendship. A true friend will not keep things away from you, but will be willing to show and expose themselves to you knowing that they can do this in confidence for you are their friend. True friendship takes time, but a boy and girl can fall in love quickly, but true love grows and develops as it gives space for friendship to mature it and make it fruitful.

True friendship will respect one another's morals and decisions, it will not ask one to do wrong when the other has stipulated boundaries and beliefs.

Let me give you an example: If you're in a relationship with someone and you tell them that because of your belief you don't desire to engage in sex outside of marriage or any sexual activities, a true friend will respect this. An individual that's not a true friend will try to persuade you with many reasons and excuses why the two of you should engage in sex or sexual activities even though they know how you feel about the situation. Remember, a friend is *one attached to another by respect or affection. One who supports or favours someone or something.* You don't want excuses, reasons or persuasions from one that is your friend, you want respect, affection, support and favour and this you will get from a true friend. Don't allow anyone to pressure or persuade you to do something that you don't desire to do. Don't be persuaded or pressured to:

- **Have sex before marriage.**
- **Get involved in drinking or drugs.**
- **Become involved in oral sex.**

When you have a true friend they will not try to persuade you to do wrong, you must separate yourself from those that try to entice you to sin. Even if you have friends that are just an associate whether they are male or female you must realize that if the two of you are going separate ways it's going to cause conflict in your Christian walk. *"For what fellowship hath righteousness with unrighteousness? And what communion hath light with darkness?" 2 Corinthians 6:14* A true friend will be there for you and will always want the best for you and your future. A true friend will love you and accept you because a true friend loves always.

11
A Boyfriend or Girlfriend

"Rejoice, O young man, in thy youth; and let thy heart cheer thee in the days of thy youth, and walk in the ways of thine heart, and in the sight of thine eyes: but know thou, that for all these things God will bring thee into judgment. Therefore remove sorrow from thy heart, and put away evil from thy flesh: for childhood and youth are vanity." Ecclesiastes 11:9-10

In your teen year's one aspect of life that will play a major role in your choices are the decisions to have a boyfriend or girlfriend. As a teen there is peer pressure to go along with the in-crowd and do what you see other teens are doing. As a teen this is the time when you want to feel grown before your time, the temptation is there to entice you to fulfill your desires and longings.

Your teen years are your most precious years and many choices are made that will affect your life. Is it wrong to have a boyfriend or girlfriend, no? However, you will have plenty of time in your life to have a boyfriend or girlfriend, but if you allow your teen years to become a time of focusing on such things it will take you off focus of the things which are most essential. Many teens squander these years and become stressed out because of boyfriend and girlfriend issues. During this time of your life if you choose to focus on a boyfriend or girlfriend you will have several before you even reach your eighteenth birthday? **The one that you think you are so in love with now want be the one that you will marry.** When you have a boyfriend or girlfriend during your teen years it is momentary and will only last for a little while. During your teen years you will have 3-5 sweethearts but you will not marry either one.

All your boyfriends and girlfriends issues during your teen years are nothing more than a fling and puppy love. To you it is very serious and we don't take it lightly that your heart is in this matter. However, your heart will be in many matters before you marry.

So what are we saying in all this?

- Boyfriends and girlfriends come and go but time is a most precious commodity that you can never get back.

- Also, this is not the time to become stressed out over boyfriend and girlfriend issues but you need to stay focused on the important issues.

- Seeking the kingdom should always be your number one priority in life. Matthew 6:33

- Your school work is very important in life and will play a major role in your future.

- Stay focused on your dreams and goals in life.

- Remember that you are a winner and being a part of the winner's circle is a choice.

If you will delay your gratifications during your teen years it will be worth your future success. There are many youthful lusts and desires during your teen years that are out to trap you and throw you off course but if you will let the Bible be your road map it will guide you in the way of success. In 2 Timothy 2:22 it says, *"Flee youthful lusts: but follow righteousness, faith, charity, peace, with them that call on the Lord out of a pure heart."*

Let the word of God be your guide and it will be *"a lamp unto your feet, and a light unto your path."* Psalms 119:105 You are a winner and winners associate with other winners, *within the mind of a winner is the attitude of gratitude and the belief that they win in life because winning is all about attitude."*

WAIT

Our Mission

Our mission is to educate, inform and inspire teens to postpone sexual activity and focus on more positive things that will equip them for a successful future. Our goal is to equip our teens with the necessary information and inspiration that will enable them to focus on their dreams, their goals and their purpose for life. We will also be an information center that will help keep youths abreast of a variety of positive opportunities that will help enhance their life as we network with other groups, clubs and organization that focus on bringing out the best in our teens.

About Us

WAIT is an organization founded by Ministers Dexter and Petula Jones that's focused on celibacy as the only 100 percent effective way to preventing pregnancy and contracting STD. WAIT stands for We Are Inactive Teens. Our goal is to educate and show teens through educational and motivational programs geared toward promoting knowledge and inspiration to wait. We do this by reinforcing self-confidence and positive values, goals, dreams, purpose and attitudes as an important prerequisite. We are available to conduct seminars and workshops at schools, churches, after-school programs, teen-retreats, etc. We also teach about relationship building, STD, pregnancy, and abstinence. The time has come to take back our teens through education, inspiration, and eventually celebration as we see our teens that are sexually active go from being sexually active to celibacy with the idea to abstain from all sexual activity until marriage. And those that are virgins remaining so until their wedding day and keeping themselves holy for the glory of God and their future life partner and soul mate in marriage.

"CELIBACY IS THE ONLY 100% EFFECTIVE WAY TO PREVENT OUT-OF-WEDLOCK PREGNANCY AND STD."

CHECK OUT OUR WEBSITE AT:
www.wewaituntilmarriage.org

CHECK OUT OUR SOCIAL WEBSITE FOR TEENS AT:
www.waituntilmarriage.socialgo.com

Email address: waituntilmarriage@yahoo.com

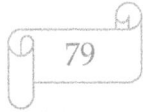

Bible Verses for Your Encouragement

- *When you feel guilty........Psalms 130:3-4, Romans 8:1-2*

- *When you feel despair.......Psalms 119:116-117, Isaiah 57:18*

- *When you are anxious........Psalms 55:22, Isaiah 41:10, Matthew 6:25-34*

- *When you are sick........Psalms 23:4, Isaiah 57:18, Matthew 8:16-17*

- *When you are tempted........Job 23:10-12, 1 Corinthians 10:13, James 1:2-4*

- *When you are confused........Psalms 32:8, Isaiah 42:16, John 8:12, 14:27, James 1:5*

- *When you are afraid........Psalms 4:8, 23:4, Isaiah 35:4, Romans 8:37-39, Hebrews 13:6*

- *When you are in need........Isaiah 58:11, 2 Corinthians 9:8, Matthew 6:25-34*

- *When you are in doubt........Psalms 34:22, Mark 11:22-26, 1 John 4:15-16,*

- *When you need comfort........Isaiah 12, 2 Corinthians 1:3-7, Psalms 91*

- *When you need an assurance of salvation........Psalms 91:14-16, John 3:14-21, 1 John 5:9-13*

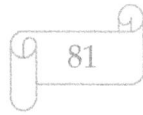

- *When you need to control your tongue........Psalms 39:1, Proverbs 10:18-20, James 3:1-12*

- *When you desire revenge........Deuteronomy 32:35, Psalms 94:1, Proverbs 25:21-22, Matthew 5:38-42*

- *When you struggle with laziness........Proverbs 6:6-11, 10:4-5, Ephesians 5:15-16*

- *When you struggle with lust........James 1:13-18, Romans 7:7-25, Galatians 5:16-17,*

- *When you struggle with addictions........Proverbs 20:1, 23:29-35, 1 Corinthians 6:12-20, Philippians 3:17-21, Romans 6:1-23*

- *When you are challenged by the devil........Ephesians 6:10-18, 2 Timothy 4:6-8, Psalms 56:1-4, Romans 8:38-39*

- *When you are angry........Genesis 4:1-12, Matthew 5:21-22, Ephesians 4:25-5:2, Psalms 4:4*

- *When your faith is being tested........Romans 5:1-11, Hebrew 10:19-25, Proverbs 3:5-8, James 1:2-4*

- *When you are tempted to avoid church........Hebrew 10:25, Acts 2:42-47, Exodus 20:8-11, Exodus 4:16-21*

- *Also, let the book of Proverbs which is a book of wisdom be your constant reading guide. There is a chapter for every day of the month, read a chapter a day and watch how God bless your life in a tremendous way.*

PRAYER FOR SALVATION:

If you need prayer for salvation we ask that you repeat the sinner's prayer below and receive Christ into your life right now.

God, according to your word I have sinned and come short of the glory of God. I stand in need of the Savior Jesus Christ. I repent of my sins and ask Jesus to come into my life. I acknowledge that I am a sinner and need to be saved. According to your word you said, "That if thou shalt confess with thy mouth the Lord Jesus, and shalt believe in thine heart that God hath raised him from the dead, thou shalt be saved. For with the heart man believeth unto righteousness; and with the mouth confession is made unto salvation." I believe that Jesus died, was resurrected and is now alive at your right hand. I ask that the blood of Jesus cleanse me from all sins and I accept Jesus into my life now. Father, I thank you for receiving me, I am now a child of God, I am now saved and my name is written in the lambs book of life, in Jesus name. Amen.

Tell us about your decision in receiving Jesus Christ as your Lord and Savior; we will get some literature out to you as soon as possible. If you have a prayer request you can email us at the email address below and we will get back with you as soon as possible.

waituntilmarriage@yahoo.com
www.wewaituntilmarriage.org

www.ingramcontent.com/pod-product-compliance
Lightning Source LLC
Chambersburg PA
CBHW071737040426
42446CB00012B/2387